The MAILBOX Gross Motor Skills for Little Learners

Active Learning With Popular Themes

- Fall
- Winter
- Spring
- Summer
- Bees
- Bugs
- Caterpillars and butterflies
- Circus
- Community helpers
- Construction
- Dinosaurs
- Farm
- Garden
- Nursery rhymes
- Ocean
- Pets
- Pond
- Transportation
- Zoo

Managing Editor: Kimberly Brugger-Murphy

Editorial Team: Becky S. Andrews, Diane Badden, Debbie Bois, Tina Borek, Marie Bortz, Janet Boyce, Tricia Kylene Brown, Kimberley Bruck, Karen A. Brudnak, Marie E. Cecchini, Patricia Conner, Elizabeth Cook, Pam Crane, Roxanne LaBell Dearman, Beth Deki, Andrea Fink, Sue Fleischmann, Sarah Foreman, Pierce Foster, Deborah Gibbone, Tazmen Hansen, Marsha Heim, Lori Z. Henry, Jennie Jensen, Debra Liverman, Kitty Lowrance, Brenda Miner, Jennifer Nunn, Keely Peasner, Tina Petersen, Gerri Primak, Mark Rainey, Greg D. Rieves, Mary Robles, Hope Rodgers, Rebecca Saunders, Donna K. Teal, Rachael Traylor, Sharon M. Tresino, Carole Watkins, Zane Williard

www.themailbox.com

©2009 The Mailbox® Books
All rights reserved.
ISBN10 #1-56234-897-3 • ISBN13 #978-156234-897-7

Printed in the United States
10 9 8 7 6 5 4 3 2 1

Table of Contents

What's Inside

Over 100 activities and pull-out helpers...

spinners

mini posters

picture cards

...for building gross-motor skills!

Gross-Motor Guide

for Three-, Four-, and Five-Year-Olds

Movements in each category progress in developmental difficulty.

Running
- runs in a fixed direction
- begins to use arms
- gains speed
- changes directions
- easily starts and stops

Jumping
- jumps in place
- jumps off a step
- jumps forward, leading with one foot
- jumps forward with both feet together

Galloping
- attempts to gallop
- gallops a few steps and then runs
- gallops smoothly for short distances

Hopping
- hops in place on one foot
- hops forward on one foot
- hops forward with increasing distance

Balancing
- walks forward along a line
- walks forward along a wide and raised surface

Climbing
- climbs stairs with assistance
- climbs a short, wide ladder
- climbs up and down stairs and ladders
- easily plays on ramps, stairs, and ladders

Throwing
- hurls a ball or beanbag
- throws underhand and overhand
- throws overhand with follow-through
- throws overhand with accuracy

Catching
- catches with arms straight out in front
- catches with elbows bent, arms in front
- catches with elbows bent, arms at side

Kicking
- makes a short kick from a standing position
- runs toward a ball and makes a short kick
- adds direction to kick
- adds height to kick

Gross-Motor Skills for Little Learners • ©The Mailbox® Books • TEC61215

Fabulous Fall!

Crunchy Leaves

Traveling

For this whole-group activity, scatter several fall leaf cutouts on your classroom floor. Then lead students in singing the song shown as they walk through the leaves. Repeat the song several times, replacing *walking* with other movements, such as *tiptoeing, stomping, marching,* and *leaping.*

(sung to the tune of "Bingo")

Oh, let's go [walking] through the leaves
And hear their leafy sounds.
Crunch, crunch, rustle, crunch,
Crunch, crunch, rustle, crunch,
Crunch, crunch, rustle, crunch!
We hear their leafy sounds!

Acorn Search

Crawling

In advance, place several brown pom-poms (acorns) around your room. Have students pretend to be squirrels and crawl around the room looking for acorns. When a child finds an acorn, have him jump up, scurry to your sand table, and then bury the acorn in the sand, much as a real squirrel would do! Encourage students to continue until all the acorns have been buried.

Pumpkin Dance

Multiple movements

Give each child an orange disposable plate (pumpkin). Then have youngsters hold their pumpkins like steering wheels and rotate them left and right as you lead them in singing the song shown. Repeat the song several times, replacing the underlined word with a different option and changing the motion accordingly.

(sung to the tune of "Pawpaw Patch")

[Rolling], [rolling] little pumpkin,
[Rolling], [rolling] little pumpkin,
[Rolling], [rolling] little pumpkin
Way down yonder in the pumpkin patch.

Continue with the following: *swaying, bouncing, turning, dancing*

Harvest Toss

Throwing

For this center, place a bushel basket a desired distance from a marked start line. Put a container of plastic fruits and vegetables near the line. A youngster stands on the line and attempts to toss the fruits and vegetables into the basket.

Floppy, Floppy Scarecrows

Bending

Cut apart the cards on page 7 and place them in a gift bag. Have a child choose a card and then identify the body part on the card. Next, lead students in reciting the rhyme shown as they bend and flop the appropriate body part. Continue in the same way with the remaining cards.

The funny, funny scarecrow
Guards the fields all day.
It waves its floppy, floppy [arms]
To scare the crows away!

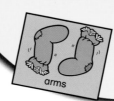

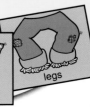

arms
head
legs

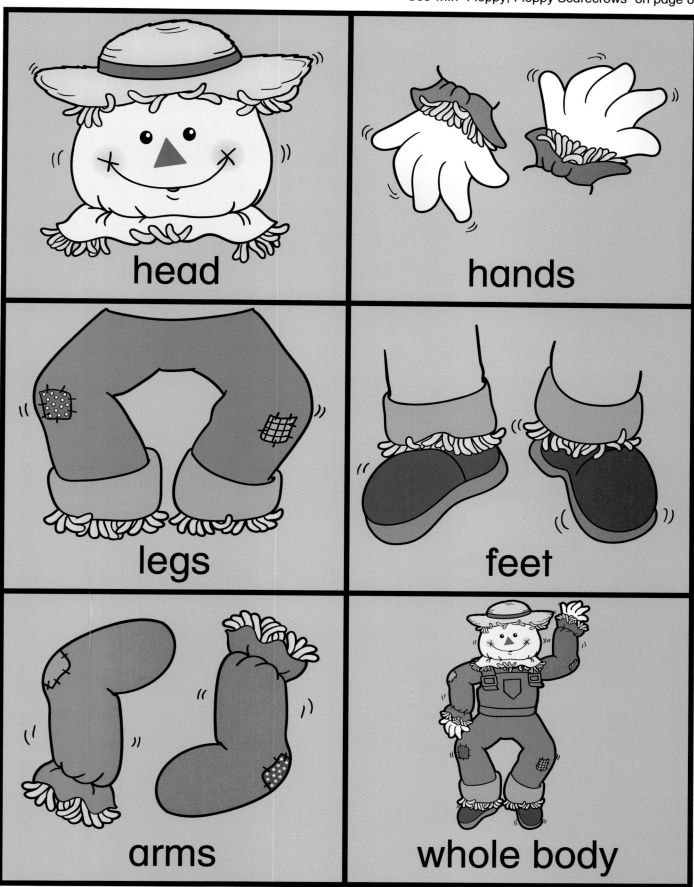

head

hands

legs

feet

arms

whole body

TEC61215

TEC61215

TEC61215

TEC61215

TEC61215

TEC61215

Wonderful Winter!

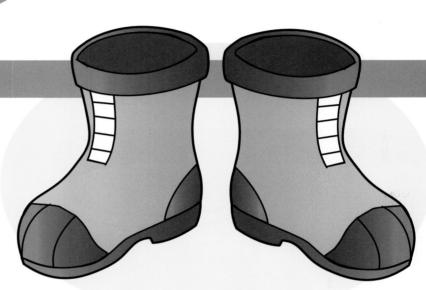

Wintry Walk

Traveling

To get little ones ready for an imaginary walk in the snow, have them pretend to put on their coats, hats, scarves, and snow boots. Then lead students around the room on a pretend walk through the snow, having them take big steps, tiptoe, shuffle their feet, and slide.

Falling Snowflakes

Multiple movements

In advance, have each youngster decorate a snowflake cutout to make a prop for this activity. Then instruct little ones to hold their snowflakes as they act out the rhyme below.

Snowflakes falling gently down.
Whirling, twirling round and round.
Snowflakes falling gently down.
Landing softly without a sound.

Snowball Catch

Tossing

For this small-group activity, give each student a funnel and a foam ball (snowball). Instruct her to hold the smaller end of the funnel and place the snowball in the larger end. Then have her gently toss the snowball in the air and attempt to catch it in the funnel. Encourage little ones to practice this activity several times.

Shoveling Snow

Bending

To prepare for this center activity, scatter cotton balls on the floor so they resemble snow and set plastic shovels and pails nearby. Students choose their shovels and bend to scoop up the snow and place it in the pails.

Winter Fun!

Multiple movements

Prepare the spinner on page 11 as shown. Then invite little ones to gather in a large open area. Have a volunteer spin the spinner and help her identify the activity. Then encourage youngsters to pantomime the activity.

Finished spinner

TEC61215

Spectacular Spring!

Puddle Jumpers

Jumping and landing

To prepare for this small-group activity, attach blue puddle cutouts to the floor. A youngster attempts to jump over each puddle and land without getting his feet "wet." To further challenge youngsters' jumping and landing skills, have students repeat the activity with several puddles in graduated sizes.

Kite Flying

Stretching

To prepare for this activity, have each child decorate a kite cutout and attach it to a craft stick. Gather youngsters in a group with their kites. Then lead your little kite fliers in performing the suggested movements while singing the song shown.

(sung to the tune of "London Bridge")

Watch my kite fly way up high
In the sky,
To and fro.
Watch my kite fly way up high.
Watch that kite go.

Stand on tiptoes and hold kite high.
Continue holding kite up high.
Sway kite from side to side.
Stand on tiptoes and hold kite high.
Sway kite from side to side.

Watch my kite glide down, down, down
Slow and low,
Near the ground.
Watch my kite glide down, down, down.
Thump! Bump! Uh-oh!

Glide kite down to the floor.
Move kite from side to side near the floor.
Continue moving kite.
Continue moving kite.
Drop kite on the floor.

Spring Shower

Tossing

For this center activity, place a large bucket (rain barrel) several feet from a marked starting line. Place a container of aluminum foil balls (raindrops) near the line. A student stands behind the line and attempts to toss the raindrops into the rain barrel. Then he counts aloud as he removes each raindrop from the barrel.

Flowers and Streamers

Dancing

Place several large colorful flower cutouts on the floor. Give each child a crepe paper streamer (or scarf) that matches a flower. Play a recording of lively music and encourage youngsters to move their streamers with dramatic flair as they dance near a flower with a corresponding color. If desired, have youngsters exchange streamers for another round of dancing.

Bunny Moves

Traveling

In advance, cut apart the cards on page 15 and place them in a basket. To begin, have youngsters pretend they are bunnies hopping in the grass as you lead them in singing the song shown. When the song is finished, invite a child to hop to the basket and pick a card. Help him identify the movement. Then lead youngsters in singing the song again, as they perform the new movement. Continue with the remaining cards.

(sung to the tune of "If You're Happy and You Know It")

There are little bunnies [hopping] in the grass.
There are little bunnies [hopping] in the grass.
They are [hopping] all around
On this pretty grassy ground.
There are little bunnies [hopping] in the grass.

crawling

tiptoeing

running

walking

marching

rolling

Sizzling Summer!

Into the Pool!

Walking

Place a blue sheet or shower curtain (pool) on the floor. Invite little ones to sit around the edge of the pool; then lead a discussion on the importance of safely walking rather than running around a real pool. Next, have students walk around the edge of the pool. After a few moments, say, "Into the pool!" and encourage youngsters to get in the pool and "splash around." Finally, direct students out of the pool and repeat the activity as time allows.

Picnic Packing

Transferring

For this center activity, place a grocery bag containing plastic food near a picnic basket. A youngster removes one food item at a time from the bag and transfers it to the basket. Encourage her to continue transferring food until the bag is empty. For a more challenging large-muscle workout, add empty condiment bottles filled with sand!

Musical Beach Ball

Passing

Play a recording of lively music and have youngsters pass a beach ball around the circle. Stop the music and then have the child holding the beach ball tell her favorite thing about summer. Repeat the process until each child has had a turn to speak.

Picnic Basket Relay

Hopping

Place at each of several stations picnic-related items, such as a cup, a paper plate, a napkin, and a plastic spoon. Place an empty basket a desired distance from each station. Separate the class into teams; then have each team line up at a station. On your signal, the first child on each team takes an item, hops to his team's basket, drops the item in, and then hops back to tag the next teammate. Continue until each team has packed all its items in its picnic basket!

Hungry Ants

Marching

For this small-group activity, cut apart the cards on page 19 and scatter them on a blanket. Have youngsters (ants) march in place around the blanket as you lead them in singing the first three lines of the song shown. Sing the fourth line, inserting a child's name and a card name. Then prompt him to pick up the appropriate card and pretend to eat the food as you lead students in singing the final lines of the song.

(sung to the tune of "The Ants Go Marching")

The ants go marching to the food—yum, yum, yum, yum.
The ants go marching to the food—yum, yum, yum, yum.
The ants go marching to the food,
And [Tyler] stops to take a [pickle].
[He] eats [his] food with a munch and a crunch
And a slurp and a gulp!
Yum, yum, yum!

TEC61215

TEC61215

TEC61215

TEC61215

TEC61215

TEC61215

Busy Bees

Straight to the Hive

Balancing

For this center activity, cut a large hive shape from bulletin board paper and display it on a classroom wall. Then attach masking tape to the floor or carpet to make a straight path that leads to the hive. Place a colorful bee cutout or a stuffed bee toy near the beginning of the path. A student picks up the bee. Then he buzzes enthusiastically as he walks along the path to the hive, taking care to stay on the tape line.

Honey Handlers

Passing

Have all your little bees quickly form a circle by holding hands. Then ask the youngsters to release hands and sit on the floor. Distribute several yellow beanbags (or something similar) to represent honey. Have the students pass the honey in the same direction around the circle as you lead them in singing the song shown. For an extra challenge, clap once to signal the children to pass the honey in the opposite direction. Other variations include quickening the tempo or alternating the method of passing between one- and two-hand passes.

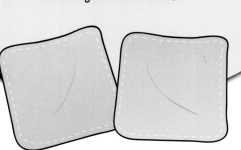

(sung to the tune of "Clementine")

Pass the honey, pass the honey.
Pass the honey around the hive!
It is gooey. It is yummy.
Pass the honey around the hive!

Follow the Queen

Multiple movements

Tell youngsters that you are the Queen Bee and it is important for all the little bees to follow you. To enhance the illusion, don a crown headband with antennae. Then do several stretches, lunges, toe touches, and other movements as youngsters follow along. If desired, have a youngster be the Queen Bee for another round of play.

Freeze, Bees!

Dancing

Keep a recording of Nikolay Rimsky-Korsakov's "The Flight of the Bumblebee" handy, and you have a honey of a movement activity at your fingertips. Simply start the music and invite students to dance and move. Stop the music at irregular intervals and say, "Freeze, bees!" As your little ones try to freeze their bodies in midmovement, applaud their gross-motor control. Next, count together to three (or another number) and restart the music.

"Bee-boppin"

Traveling

Students can have hours of fun playing this simple game! Cut out the direction cards on page 23 and then tape one card to each side of a small cube-shaped box. To play, specify a traveling movement, such as tiptoeing; then invite a youngster to roll the cube. Help the child count the dots and interpret the pictured directions. Then have students move accordingly. Play several rounds of this fun game with different traveling movements.

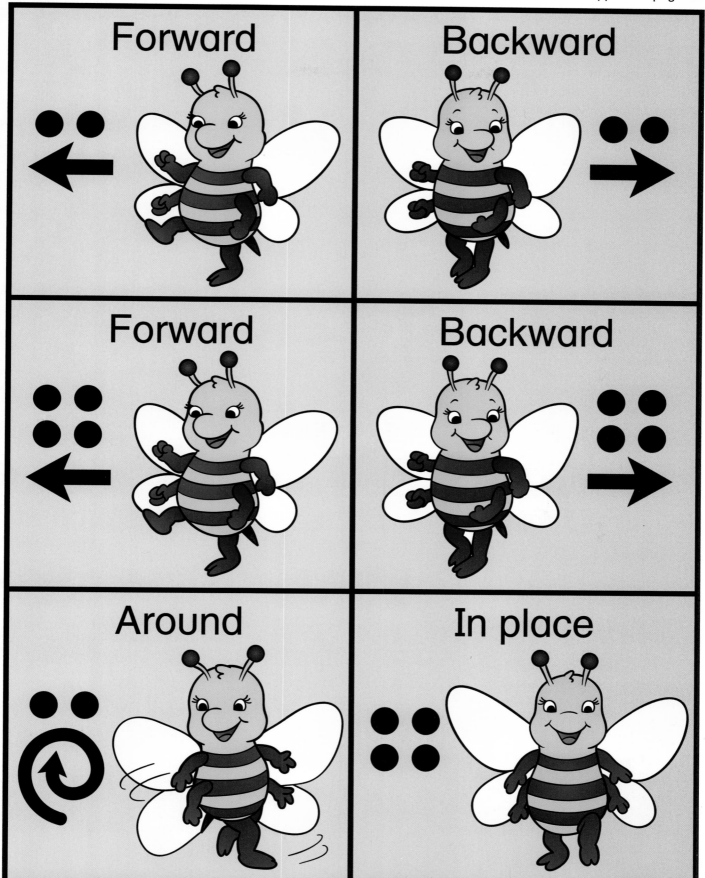

Forward

Backward

Forward

Backward

Around

In place

Going Buggy!

Balancing Bugs

Multiple movements

For this relay, direct youngsters to form two lines. Have the first child in each line balance a plastic bug on a flyswatter. At your signal, the two students walk their bugs to a designated turnaround spot and then walk back to the line. When they return, they pass the swatters to the next students. Play continues until each student has had a turn.

Dance of the Bugs

Traveling

Lead little ones in singing the song shown as they crawl about like ladybugs. Have students sing additional verses of the song, replacing the bug name and making appropriate movements.

(sung to the tune of "The Mulberry Bush")

This is the way the [ladybug crawls].
[Ladybug crawls], [ladybug crawls].
This is the way the [ladybug crawls]
All around the garden.

Continue with the following: *bumblebee buzzes, butterfly flutters, tiny ant marches, grasshopper hops*

Pest Control

Bending

For this center activity, place plastic bugs around your classroom and provide tongs and a plastic container. If desired, also provide a nametag labeled "Pest Control." A child dons the nametag and then walks about the room, bending down and using the tongs to pick up the bugs and place them in the container.

Pest Control

Centipede Travel

Walking

Have students form a line behind you. Then encourage each child to hold the shoulders of the person in front of him. Explain to youngsters that they are going to pretend to be a long bug called a centipede. Then lead students around the room, encouraging them to take tiny bug steps!

Colorful Grasshoppers

Jumping

Cut apart the grasshopper cards on page 27. To begin, gather youngsters in a circle and give each child a square of construction paper to match one of the grasshopper colors. Hold up a grasshopper card and invite each student with a matching paper to step into the circle and jump around like a grasshopper. After a minute of jumping, have the students move back to their spots in the circle. Continue with the remaining grasshopper cards.

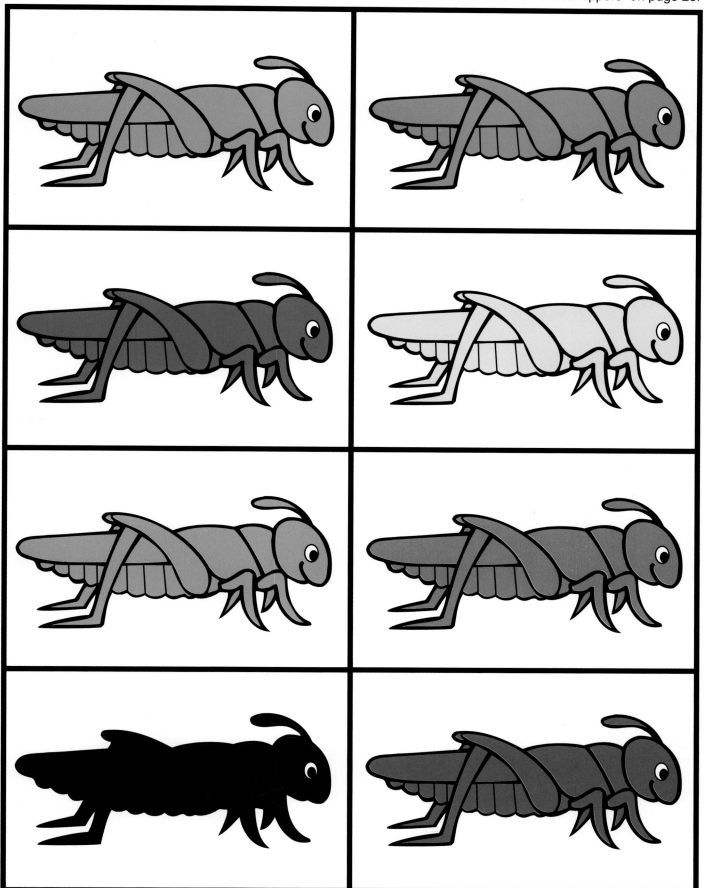

TEC61215

TEC61215

TEC61215

TEC61215

TEC61215

TEC61215

TEC61215

TEC61215

Caterpillars and Butterflies

Caterpillar Crawl

Crawling

For this small-group activity, attach an oversize leaf cutout to the floor. Have each child pretend she is a caterpillar crawling around looking for a leaf to eat. Then give directions such as "Crawl around the leaf," "Crawl beside the leaf," and "Crawl across the leaf." End the activity by having each of your little caterpillars curl up and pretend to be asleep in a chrysalis.

Butterfly Garden

Skipping

For this whole-group activity, scatter several colorful flower cutouts in an open area. Give each child a butterfly stick puppet that matches the color of a flower. Have youngsters hold their butterflies in the air and skip around. After a few moments, signal students to skip to a flower that is a matching color. After checking to see that each child has made a match, have her exchange her butterfly with a classmate; then begin the activity again.

Butterfly, Butterfly

Multiple movements

Have students pretend to be butterflies when they perform this fun action rhyme.

Butterfly, butterfly, fly real slow.	Flap arms and walk slowly.
Butterfly, butterfly, fly real low.	Bend down low.
Butterfly, butterfly, fly with haste.	Flap arms and walk quickly.
Butterfly, butterfly, take a taste.	Bend over and pretend to sip nectar.
Butterfly, butterfly, fly up high.	Stand on tiptoes; stretch arms high.
Butterfly, butterfly, wave goodbye!	Hold arms out at sides; flutter hands.

Graceful Butterflies

Balancing

This activity is handy for assessing balance. To prepare, attach a large flower cutout to the floor; then add a masking tape stem to the flower. Cut out the cards on page 31 and use them as visual references while explaining this activity to your youngsters. To begin, have a student pretend he is a butterfly and walk heel to toe along the stem to the flower. Next, have him stand on the flower with his arms out and balance on one foot. Then have him repeat the movement with the opposite foot.

Walking Heel to Toe

Balancing on One Foot

Walking Heel to Toe

Balancing on One Foot

TEC61215

TEC61215

At the Circus

On the Tightrope

Balancing

For this center activity, attach masking tape to the floor so it resembles a tightrope and set out a few props, such as swimming pool noodles, long scarves, and a small umbrella. A student chooses a prop and holds it as he carefully walks along the tightrope. He repeats the process with other props.

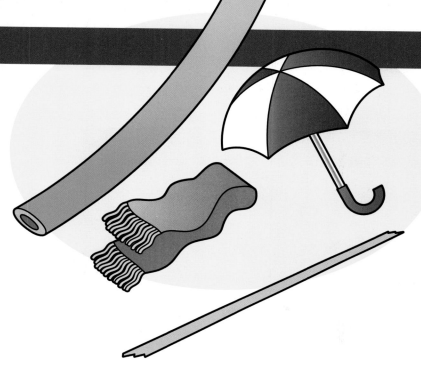

(sung to the tune of "My Bonnie Lies Over the Ocean")

I am a preschool trapeze artist.
I climb up a ladder so high.
I hold the trapeze bar quite tightly.
And then I get ready to fly!
Swinging, swinging,
I swing to and fro; to and fro I go.
Swinging, swinging,
And then it is time to let go!

Point to self.
Pretend to climb a ladder.
Hold arms up and pretend to grasp bar.
Hold arms up and jump.
Sway forward and backward.

Drop to a crouch and bounce as if
    hitting a net.

Trapeze Artists

Multiple movements

Gather youngsters in your large-group area. Then lead them in the action song shown.

Boogie Like a Bear

Dancing

To begin, invite volunteers to share their favorite dance moves. Then pretend to be the circus ringleader and announce the dancing bear act. Play a recording of lively music and invite little ones to pretend to be dancing bears at the circus. Change songs several times, encouraging little ones to try a variety of dance moves.

Seal Tricks

Balancing

Tell students that they are trained seals at the circus. Give each student a beanbag. Then say "head" and have students balance their beanbags on their heads. Say "stop" and have the youngsters drop the beanbags and slap their arms together as if they were flippers. Repeat the activity using other body parts, such as shoulder, elbow, hand (back and palm), and foot.

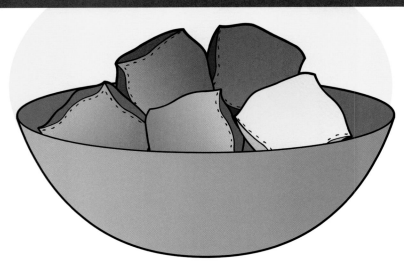

And in This Ring

Multiple movements

Cut apart the cards on page 35 and place them in a hat. Have a student take a card from the hat and name the circus performer. Then invite youngsters to act like that performer. Continue in the same way with the remaining cards.

TEC61215

TEC61215

TEC61215

TEC61215

TEC61215

TEC61215

Community Helpers

Hot Pot!

Passing

Have your little cooks stand in a circle. Remove one student (the head chef) from the circle and have him stand with his back to the remaining students. Hand a cook a two-handled pot. Have him twist his body to pass the pot to the next cook. Have youngsters continue to pass the pot until the head chef says, "Hot pot!" The cook holding the pot switches places with the head chef and play continues.

Delivering the News

Throwing

For this center activity, individually roll several newspapers and place a rubber band around each paper. Put the papers in a bag with a shoulder strap. Draw houses on a length of bulletin board paper and attach the paper to a wall. When a student visits the center, he "delivers" the papers by throwing a paper in front of each house. After delivering all the papers, he collects them and returns them to the bag for the next child to use.

Waiting Tables

Balancing

To prepare for this whole-group activity, place a disposable plate and cup on a plastic tray. Have little ones sit at tables and pretend they are restaurant patrons. Hand the tray to a child (food server) and instruct her to carry the tray around the tables, being careful not to drop the plate or cup. Then have her set the tray in front of a classmate. The classmate becomes the food server and play continues until each student has had a turn.

Making Deliveries

Multiple movements

To make a delivery truck, place two student chairs in front of an empty water table. Provide boxes, a clipboard with paper, a pencil, and keys on a ring. When students visit the center, they load the boxes into the truck. Then they pretend to drive to different locations and deliver each box.

Construction Worker Song

Multiple movements

Cut apart the cards on page 39. Have a child choose a card and help him describe the action. Then lead youngsters in singing the song shown, substituting the appropriate action, and encourage students to pantomime the action. Have students repeat the process for each remaining card.

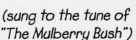
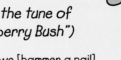

(sung to the tune of "The Mulberry Bush")

This is the way we [hammer a nail],
[Hammer a nail], [hammer a nail].
This is the way we [hammer a nail]
Like a construction worker.

saw a board

tighten a screw

hammer a nail

climb a ladder

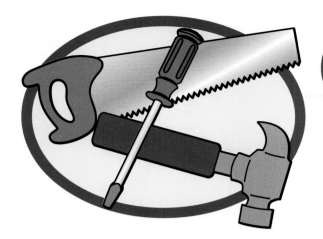

Construction Time

Construction Beam

Balancing

For this small-group activity, use masking tape to make a straight path (beam) on your floor. Place a container of plastic tools and an empty toolbox at opposite ends of the beam. In turn, have each child pick a tool from the container, walk across the beam, and then place the tool in the toolbox.

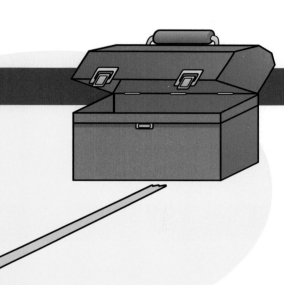

I Can Pound

I can pound with one hammer, one hammer, one hammer.
I can pound with two hammers, two hammers, two hammers.
I can pound with three hammers, three hammers, three hammers.
I can pound with four hammers, four hammers, four hammers.
I can pound with five hammers, five hammers, five hammers.
And then I need a rest!

Multiple movements

For this whole-group activity, have students stand. As youngsters recite the first line of the rhyme, have them bend one arm and move it like they are pounding with a hammer. During the second line, encourage them to repeat the motion with both arms. Have youngsters continue the arm motion during the third line while they stamp one foot. Then, during the fourth line, prompt them to move their arms and stamp both feet. Finally, have them lie on the floor and rest during the final line.

Bulldozer or Jackhammer?

Multiple movements

Discuss with youngsters the purposes of a jackhammer and a bulldozer. Prompt youngsters to bounce up and down like jackhammers and then crawl on the floor with their hands in front of them like bulldozers. Next, play a recording of upbeat music and say "jackhammer," prompting youngsters to move like jackhammers to the music. Then call out "bulldozer" and have them drop to the floor and move like bulldozers. Continue in the same way, alternating movements throughout the song.

Sanding Center

Pushing and pulling

To prepare, attach sandpaper to one side of each of several wooden blocks. Put the sanding blocks on a covered surface along with thick sheets of cardboard. Have a youngster don a pair of safety goggles. Then instruct him to use a push-and-pull motion to sand a cardboard sheet with a sanding block.

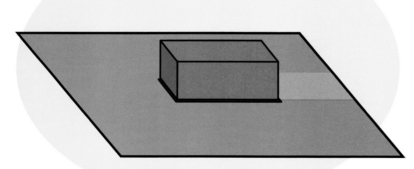

Using Tools

Multiple movements

Cut apart the cards on page 43 and place them in a toolbox. Have a child draw a card and then help her name the tool. Ask youngsters how people might use this tool. Then prompt students to pantomime using the tool, encouraging large exaggerated movements.

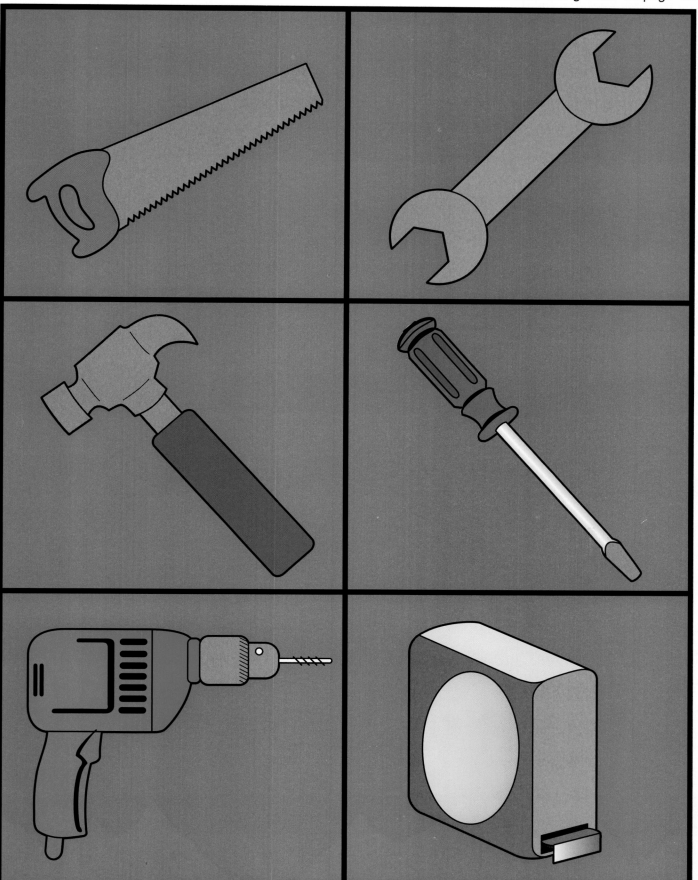

TEC61215

TEC61215

TEC61215

TEC61215

TEC61215

TEC61215

TEC61215

TEC61215

Dinosaur Moves

Dino Stomp

Stomping

Arrange numbered rock cutouts in a circle on your floor, making sure that each number is represented several times. Then have each child stand behind a rock. Say, "Dino stomp!" and have students stomp around the rocks. Then call out, "Dino stop!" to signal each student to stand behind a rock. Next, name a number. Each child standing behind the corresponding number stomps his feet that many times. Continue play for several rounds.

Dinosaur Hopscotch

Hopping

For this small-group game, draw a hopscotch grid on a paved surface (or use tape to make a grid indoors). Place a large bone cutout in the area beyond the final boxes (the dinosaur swamp). A child hops to the swamp using one or two feet, picks up the bone, and then hops back and hands it to the next child. The new player hops to the swamp, leaves the bone, and then hops back. Play continues until each child has had a turn.

Dinosaur Hunt

Traveling

To prepare for this small-group activity, arrange a simple obstacle course in your classroom or outdoor play area that will require movements such as climbing, crawling, jumping, walking, and balancing; then hide a toy dinosaur at the end of the course. Tell students a dinosaur is hiding somewhere in the area; then lead small groups of youngsters through the obstacle course to help them find the dinosaur.

Giant Steps!

Walking

Make two identical sets of colorful dinosaur cutouts. Then divide the class in half and have teams stand facing each other several yards apart. Pass out a set of dinosaurs to the youngsters on each team. Announce a color and have each student with a corresponding dinosaur hold it in the air. After confirming the colors, have each child holding up his dinosaur take giant dinosaur steps to switch places with a student in the opposite row. Continue until each child has switched rows.

On the Move

Multiple movements

For this whole-group activity, assemble the spinner from page 47. Have a child spin the spinner and identify the dinosaur as one that flies, walks on two legs, swims, or walks on four legs. Have youngsters move about the room like that dinosaur until you say to stop. Then play another round of the game.

Pteranodon

Triceratops

Tyrannosaur

Plesiosaur

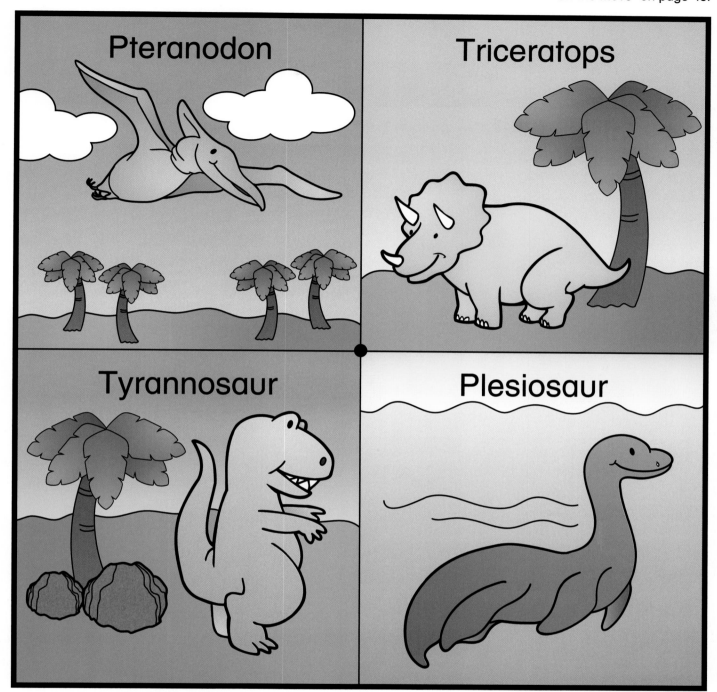

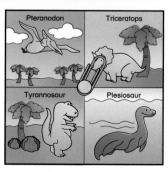

Finished Spinner

TEC61215

Down on the Farm

Ready to Hatch

Multiple movements

Have each student curl up on the floor and pretend to be a chick in an egg. To help each chick hatch, instruct her to move her head up and down as if pecking the shell with her beak. Next, have her bend her elbows (wings) and push them up and down to poke through the shell. Then have her stretch her legs, stand, and wiggle vigorously to free herself from the egg. Finally, have your little chicks shake their feathers dry and then walk to and fro saying, "Peep."

Farm Action

Traveling

For this whole-group activity, lead students in singing the song shown as they gallop around the room pretending to be horses. Then repeat the song several times, substituting the underlined words with the additional phrases and having youngsters move accordingly.

(sung to the tune of "The Farmer in the Dell")

The [horses gallop around].
The [horses gallop around].
It's fun down on the farm.
The [horses gallop around].

Continue with the following:
pigs roll in the mud
ducks waddle about
chicks peck at the seeds

Gathering Eggs

Passing

Have youngsters form a line. Then put a sterilized egg carton near the front of the line and a basket of plastic eggs near the back of the line. To begin, make a chicken sound to signal the last child to pass an egg to the child in front of him, who then retrieves the egg from over her head. Youngsters continue to pass the egg overhead; then the child at the front of the line puts the egg in the egg carton. Students continue until all the eggs are in the carton.

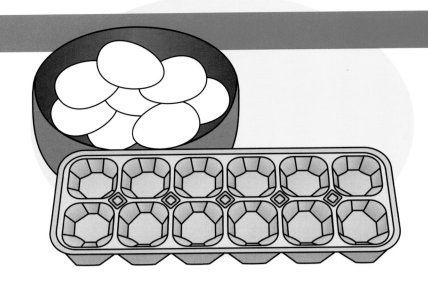

Flock of Sheep

Chasing and fleeing

Gather youngsters in a large open area. Invite a child to pretend to be a sheepdog. Have the remaining youngsters pretend to be sheep and stand in a flock a short distance away. On your signal, the dog chases the flock, trying to tag one of the sheep. If a sheep is tagged, she becomes the new sheepdog. Then the sheep form a new flock, and the game begins again.

Barnyard Banter

Traveling

Cut apart the cards on page 51 and attach each one to a simple barn cutout. Scatter the barns in an open area. To begin, have youngsters walk in a circle around the barns as you play a recording of lively music. When you stop the music, have each child stand near a barn and make the sound of the corresponding animal. Repeat the activity several times, using other movements such as marching, hopping, sidestepping, and tiptoeing.

Gorgeous Gardens

Colorful Flowers

Jumping

Tell youngsters they are going to pretend to be seeds. Then have them crouch in your large-group area. Spray a plant mister over the group of youngsters and say, "It's raining on the little seeds." Then say, "Now the sun is shining," and have students jump into a standing position as if they have grown into flowers. Repeat the activity several times.

Little Gardeners

Multiple movements

Lead your little gardeners in singing and acting out this engaging song!

(sung to the tune of "I've Been Working on the Railroad")

I've been working in my garden,
Helping my plants grow.
I've been working in my garden
With my shovel, rake, and hoe.
See the pretty flowers growing,
Short and tall ones too.
They need water, food, and sunshine
And lots of growing room!

Pantomime digging with a shovel.

Pantomime raking.

Stand on tiptoes and stretch arms up.
Touch the floor; then stretch up high.
Make a circle with arms (sun).
Move arms back and forth parallel to floor.

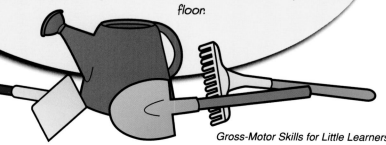

Wiggle Worms

Crawling

Divide the class into several teams. Have all children but one on each team stand in line and spread their feet apart to create a tunnel. Encourage each remaining team member to crawl through the tunnel like a worm and then stand like his teammates on the opposite side. The child at the beginning of the tunnel becomes the next worm.

Musical Garden

Traveling

Scatter a supply of die-cut flowers on your floor. Play music and have students dance through the flower garden, trying not to step on the flowers. Stop the music periodically and announce other movements for students to perform, such as tiptoeing, hopping, marching, and jumping.

Flower Relay

Galloping

Remove the poster on page 55 and display it in your classroom. Use the poster to explain and demonstrate how to gallop. Then give each child a plastic flower and have students stand in a line. Place a flowerpot at a desired distance from the line. On your signal, the first child gallops to the flowerpot, deposits the flower, and then runs back to tag the next child in line. Play continues until all the flowers are in the pot.

Galloping

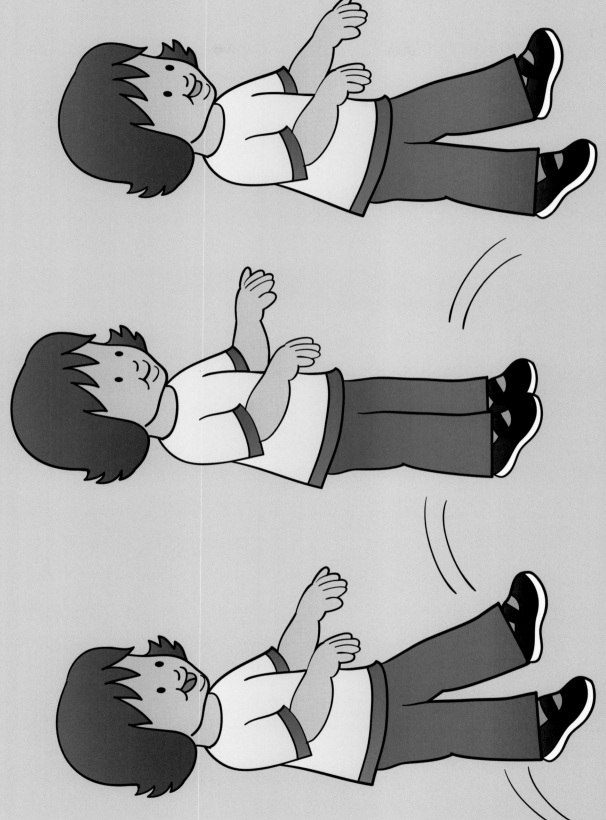

Nursery Rhymes

One Steep Hill

Walking

For this dramatization of "Jack and Jill," make a hill outline on the floor with masking tape. Invite two children to play the roles of Jack and Jill; then give each child a plastic pail. Lead the remaining youngsters in reciting the nursery rhyme as the pair walk heel to toe along the tape to the top of the hill. At the appropriate time, have Jack tumble (roll) down the opposite side of the hill with Jill tumbling down shortly after. For an added challenge, have youngsters walk up the hill backward!

Ticktock

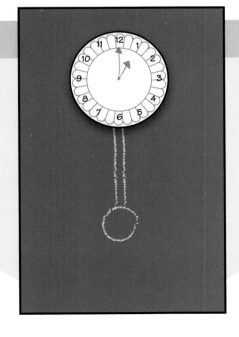

Traveling

To prepare for this "Hickory Dickory Dock" activity, place a simple grandfather clock craft on your floor. In turn, invite volunteers to stand near the bottom of the clock to play the role of the mouse. Have each child run up one side of the clock and then down the other as you lead the rest of the class in reciting "Hickory Dickory Dock." For added interest, replace *ran* with other movements, such as *tiptoed, crawled,* and *hopped.*

Twinkle, Twinkle

Multiple movements

For this activity, give each child a star stick puppet that has been covered with aluminum foil. To begin, turn off the lights. Have each child crouch and hold her star in front of her. Next, shine a flashlight over the stars; then lead youngsters in singing "Twinkle, Twinkle, Little Star." When you sing "Up above the world so high," have each child slowly stand, hold her star in the air, and then sway from side to side. To end the song, have youngsters return to a crouched position.

Jumping

Jump, Jack, Jump!

Jumping and landing

Attach yellow tissue paper to the top of a block (appropriately sized for little ones to jump over) so it resembles a candle. Remove the mini poster on page 59 and use it to review the steps of jumping. Then have a youngster pretend to be Jack. Lead the students in reciting "Jack Be Nimble" as Jack jumps over the candle. Continue until each child has had a turn to play Jack.

Jumping

Gross-Motor Skills for Little Learners • ©The Mailbox® Books • TEC61215

Awesome Ocean

Shark Tag

Running

Mark off a large open area (ocean). Have one child (shark) stand in the center of the ocean and the remaining youngsters (fish) stand at one end. To play, the shark calls out, "One, two, three! Swim past me!" Then the fish run past the shark to the opposite side of the ocean. If the shark tags a fish, the fish becomes a shark as well. The game continues in the same way until each fish becomes a shark.

One, two, three! Swim past me!

Surfing the Waves

Multiple movements

For this small-group activity, place several surfboard cutouts on the floor. Have each student stand on a surfboard; then lead students in singing the song shown as they each bend their knees pretending to surf the ocean waves. Repeat the song several times, replacing *bend* with other movements, such as *twist, turn,* and *crouch.*

(sung to the tune of "The Farmer in the Dell")

We [bend] to surf the waves.
We [bend] to surf the waves.
High, low, a-surfing we go.
We [bend] to surf the waves!

Beach Ball Bounce

Pushing

Have students sit in a circle and then give a child a beach ball. Encourage the child to call out the name of a classmate and push the ball so it rolls to the classmate. Have the classmate repeat the process. Students continue to play the game until each child receives and pushes the ball.

Sand Pail Catch

Throwing and catching

For this partner activity, give one child a plastic sand pail and the remaining child a sponge; then have the pair stand several feet apart. The child with the sponge throws it to his partner, who attempts to catch it in the pail. Then the partners switch. For some added fun, have youngsters throw a wet sponge!

School of Fish

Tossing

In advance, assemble the spinner from page 63. Place a sheet of blue bulletin board paper (ocean) on the floor along with a container of eight craft foam fish cutouts. Have a child spin the spinner and identify the number. Then have her toss the corresponding number of fish onto the ocean. After confirming that she is correct, have her put the fish back in the pail.

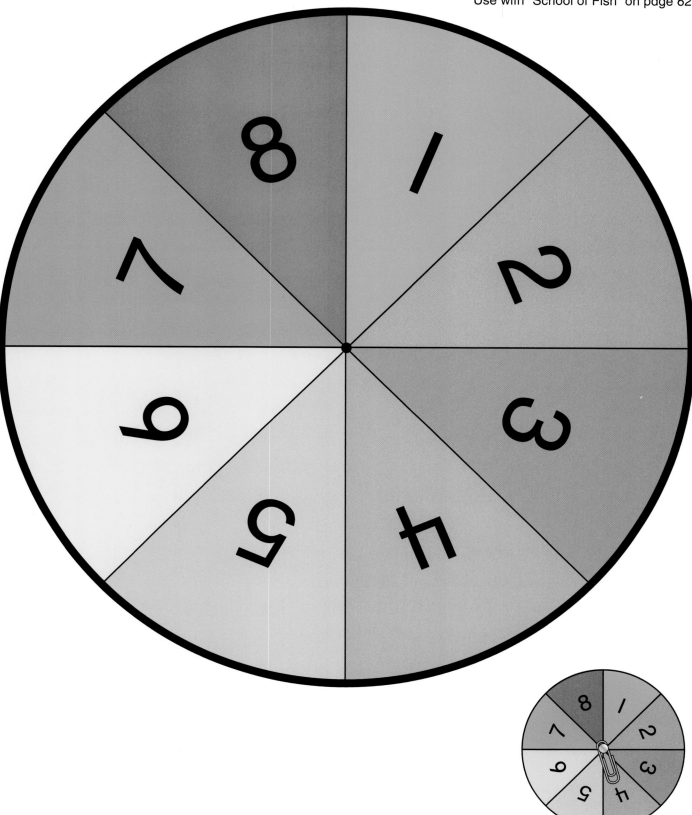

Finished Spinner

TEC61215

Perky Pets

Kitty's Dinner

Passing

For this whole-group activity, partially fill a small plastic bowl with cereal pieces (cat food). Have youngsters sit in a circle. Then hand the bowl to a child. Prompt him to meow and then pass the bowl to his neighbor, who meows in return. Have students continue passing the bowl until it makes a complete revolution around the circle.

In Fishy's Bowl

Traveling

Invite each youngster to pretend she is a fish who is enjoying a pleasant swim around her fishbowl. Announce a direction—such as forward, backward, to the side, or in circles—and instruct her to swim in the stated direction. Play continues for several rounds.

Feather's Folly

Sidestepping, jumping

To prepare this center, affix to your floor several parallel lengths of masking tape (bird perches). A child stands at one end of a perch. Then he sidesteps to the opposite end, being careful to keep both feet on the perch. When he reaches the end, he jumps to a different perch and repeats the activity.

Fluffy's Workout

Pushing

In advance, place a small stuffed animal in a hamster's exercise ball. Sit in a circle with your students and roll the ball to a child. Instruct her to stop the ball, state the name she would give to a pet hamster, and then roll the ball to a classmate. Continue until each student has had a turn.

Fido's Bath

Stretching

Cut apart the cards on page 67 and place them in a bag. Tell students that they are going to be dog washers and they are all washing very large dogs! Give each child a sponge. Then have a student choose a card from the bag and identify the part of the dog that needs to be washed, such as the dog's ears. Tell students to stretch way up high to wash the dog's ears until they're very clean. Repeat the process for each card, having students stretch in different directions to wash the oversize dog. Throughout the activity, tell students that the dog is trying to get out of the bathtub and encourage them to use all their strength to hold it in place.

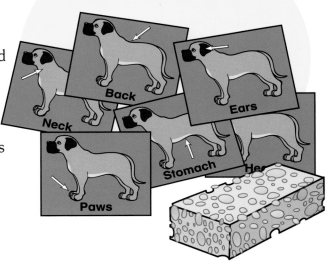

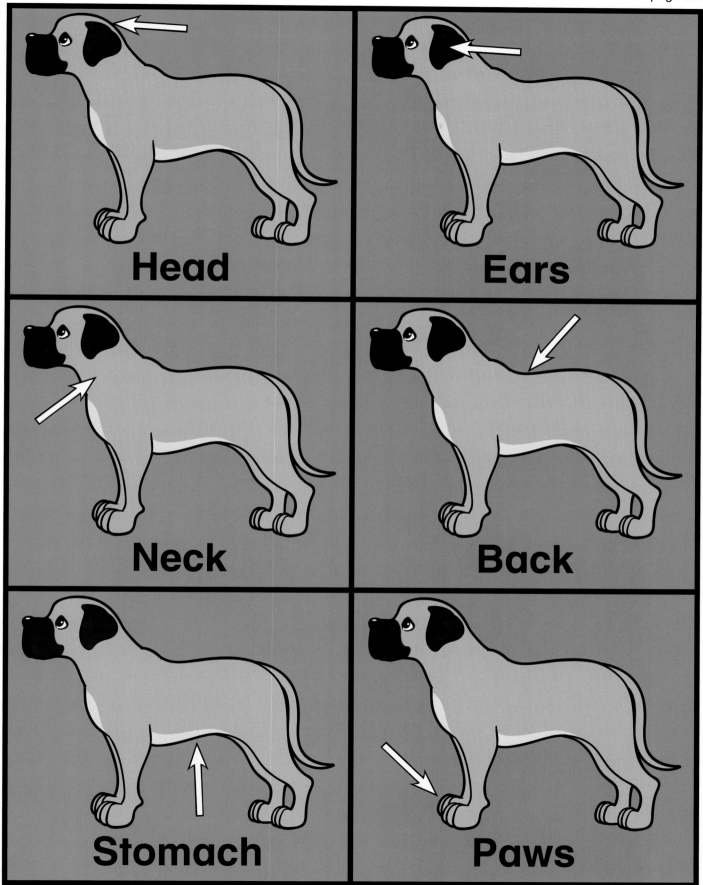

Head

Ears

Neck

Back

Stomach

Paws

Pleasing Pond

Pond Crossing

Traveling

For this center activity, make a pond outline on your classroom floor using blue yarn. Attach inside the pond several large rock cutouts and a log cutout. Youngsters cross the pond using different movements, such as walking heel-to-toe or tiptoeing across the log; stepping, jumping, or hopping on one foot from rock to rock; and leaping.

Lily Pad Pounce

Hopping

In advance, label lily pad cutouts with numbers from 1 to 10. Attach the lily pads to your floor in numerical order. Place a corresponding set of number cards in a bag. To begin, invite a child to be the frog. Lead the rest of the group in reciting the chant shown. At the end of the chant, pick a card from the bag and have students identify the number. Then lead youngsters in counting along as the frog hops to each lily pad in order, stopping at the chosen number. Play several rounds of this game.

Little frog, little frog,
Hop, hop, hop!
This is the number
Where you'll stop!

Parachute Play

Traveling

Gather little ones around a parachute (or a bedsheet). Assign each child one of the following pond critter names: fish, frog, turtle, or duck. To play, help students lift the parachute high in the air. Call out, "[Swim, fish, swim]!" Then have each fish "swim" under the parachute to the opposite side. Repeat the activity several times, replacing the underlined words with *Hop, frog, hop; Crawl, turtle, crawl;* and *Waddle, duck, waddle.*

Ring Around the Critters

Tossing

Place a large pond cutout on your classroom floor. Place several small toy pond critters on the cutout and have a container of plastic rings nearby. (If plastic rings are not available, trim the centers from paper plates.) A youngster stands at the *edge* of the pond and attempts to toss a ring around each animal.

Pond Pantomimes

Multiple movements

Cut apart the animal picture cards on page 71. Show youngsters each card, prompting students to identify the critter and describe how it moves. Next, secretly show a volunteer one of the cards. Then have her silently demonstrate to the class how the pictured critter moves. Have the remaining youngsters guess what the critter is. Finally, have the entire class pretend to be the critter. Repeat the activity with each remaining card, encouraging students to perform the suggestions shown.

Terrific Transportation

Going to Grandma's House

Multiple movements

Tell youngsters a story about an imaginary trip to Grandma's house that includes several forms of transportation. Encourage students to add actions to the story, such as "flying" around the room like a plane, bouncing up and down as if riding in a car over a bumpy road, "sailing" smoothly in a boat, and marching up a steep hill.

Driving the Bus

Twisting

Give each of your little bus drivers a paper plate (steering wheel). Have students act out driving a bus as you lead them in singing the song shown. Repeat the song several times, replacing the underlined words with a different option each time.

(sung to the tune of "The Mulberry Bush")

This is the way we [drive the bus].
[Drive the bus]. [drive the bus].
This is the way we [drive the bus]
All through the great big city.

Continue with the following: *make a right turn,
make a left turn, beep the horn, stop the bus,
open the door*

Crossing the Stream

Bending

Instruct partners to sit in an imaginary rowboat facing each other. Place a stuffed toy bear between each pair of students. Have the partners hold hands and rock forward and backward to imitate rowing a boat. As little ones row their boats, lead them in singing the song.

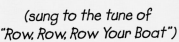

(sung to the tune of "Row, Row, Row Your Boat")

Row, row, row the bear
Across the flowing stream.
Merrily, merrily, merrily, merrily,
We make quite a team!

Row, row, row the bear
To the other side.
Merrily, merrily, merrily, merrily,
Oh my, what a ride!

(sung to the tune of "The Farmer in the Dell")

We're going on a trip.
We'll get there in a [car].
Up and down, we'll ride around.
We'll get there in a [car].

Let's Take a Trip

Multiple movements

Encourage little ones to move about the room as if they were cars while they sing the song several times. Ask a volunteer to name another form of transportation. Then repeat the song, replacing the form of transportation and encouraging youngsters to move appropriately.

Things That Go

Balancing

To prepare for this center activity, attach masking tape to the floor to make a straight line, a curved line, and a zigzag line. Prepare the spinner on page 75 and place it at the center. A student spins the spinner and then pretends to be the displayed mode of transportation as he moves along the line of his choice, being careful to keep both feet on the line.

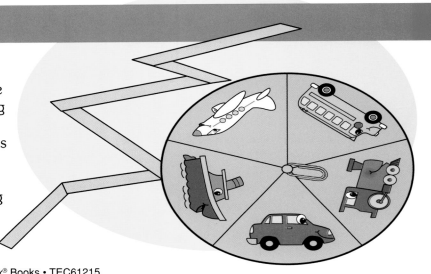

Finished Spinner

TEC61215

Zoo Fun!

Monkey Munch

Multiple movements

Arrange chairs in a large square (cage) with the seats facing in. Place a banana cutout labeled with a desired letter under each chair. Gather youngsters in the cage. Have each child pretend to be a monkey using movements such as jumping, hopping, bending, swaying, and moving her arms up and down. Next, chant, "Monkey munch! It's time for lunch!" Then have each child take a seat and remove the banana from under her chair. In turn, have each student identify the letter and then place the banana back under the chair.

Peanut Pass

Passing

Divide the students into two teams. Then have team members stand side by side with space between them. Place an equal number of large craft foam peanut cutouts at one end of each line and a pail at the opposite end. Have each student pretend to be an elephant by extending his arms forward so they resemble a trunk. On your signal, have the elephants use their trunks to pass the peanut down the line. Then have the last elephant in line drop the peanut in the pail. Continue until each team has all of its peanuts in its pail.

Tallest of All!

Walking

Explain to students that a giraffe is the tallest of all animals, with most adult males standing about 17 feet tall and their legs measuring about six feet long! Play a recording of slow music and encourage youngsters to walk about the room as giraffes would walk, using exaggerated long strides.

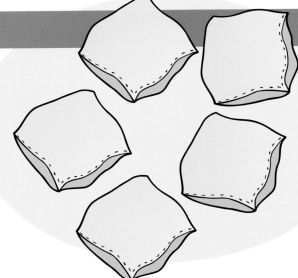

Banana Ball

Throwing and catching

For this partner game, have two students stand several feet apart. Then give one child a yellow beanbag (banana). To play, the student throws the banana to his partner. If the child catches it, both youngsters jump around pretending to be monkeys. If the youngster does not catch the banana, he simply throws it back. Play continues for several rounds.

Feeding Time at the Zoo!

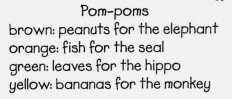

Tossing

For this center, cut apart the cards on page 79. Attach a pom-pom to each card (see color list shown); then attach each card to a separate pail. Place the pails on the floor several feet from a marked start line. Put a container of large brown, orange, green, and yellow pom-poms near the line. A child stands on the line and attempts to toss each pom-pom into a corresponding pail to feed the animals.

Pom-poms
brown: peanuts for the elephant
orange: fish for the seal
green: leaves for the hippo
yellow: bananas for the monkey

TEC61215

TEC61215

TEC61215

TEC61215